Vegan Barbecues and Buffets

Also by Linda Majzlik

Festive Food for Vegetarians (1991)
Party Food for Vegetarians (1995)
Vegan Dinner Parties (1998)

Vegan Barbecues and Buffets

Linda Majzlik

JON CARPENTER

Our books may be ordered from bookshops or (post free) from
Jon Carpenter Publishing, 2 The Spendlove Centre, Charlbury, OX7 3PQ

Please send for our free catalogue

Credit card orders should be phoned or faxed to 01689 870437
or 01608 811969

In **North America** our distributor is Paul and Company

In **Australia** and **New Zealand** our distributor is Envirobook

In **South Africa** our distributor is New Horizon Distributors

First published in 1999 by
Jon Carpenter Publishing
2, The Spendlove Centre, Charlbury, Oxfordshire OX7 3PQ
☎ 01608 811969

ISBN 1 897766 55 6

Cover design by Sarah Tyzack. Cover illustration by Mark Blanford

Printed in England by J. W. Arrowsmith Ltd., Bristol BS3 2NT
Cover printed by KMS Litho, Hook Norton OX15 5NP

Introduction

ONCE IT GETS WARMER WE START TO THINK ABOUT ENTERTAINING and eating outside, and when it comes to barbecues vegans certainly don't have to miss out, as the following recipes show. Add some salads, dips and savouries, and you have a veritable alfresco feast.

For larger numbers of guests you may prefer to lay on a buffet spread, whether inside or out, and a selection of savoury loaves, patés, pastries, rice timbales, little savouries and salads, together with dips and spreads, should tempt the most discerning palate. A lot of the preparation can be done in advance, with many of the foods suitable for freezing, while others can be made the day before and kept in the fridge. With just a few salads, desserts and spreads to make on the day, you should be able to enjoy the occasion as much as your guests and not be tied to the kitchen.

How much food to serve can be tricky, as many people will be tempted to eat more than usual at barbecues and buffets, especially when the food looks so appetising. So allow enough for guests to come back for another helping. Desserts are always popular, with many people wanting to sample more than one!

Linda Majzlik
Swanton Morley

BARBECUES

A LL OF THE FOLLOWING CAN BE PREPARED IN ADVANCE AND BE ready to cook when guests arrive, but remember to start off the jacket potatoes earlier as they take longer. Serve the barbecued foods with a selection of salads, dips and savouries from the other sections.

Curried courgette and walnut burgers *Makes 8*

8oz/225g courgette, grated

2oz/50g walnuts, grated

2oz/50g fresh wholemeal breadcrumbs

2oz/50g wholemeal flour

1oz/25g sultanas, chopped

1oz/25g soya flour

1 onion, peeled and grated

1 garlic clove, crushed

4 tablespoons water

1 rounded teaspoon curry paste

3 cardamoms, husked and the seeds separated

black pepper

oatbran

sunflower oil

Put the courgette, walnuts, breadcrumbs, flour, sultanas, onion, garlic and cardamom seeds in a mixing bowl and combine well. Mix the curry paste with the water, add the soya flour and stir until smooth. Add to the courgette and walnut mixture and season with black pepper. Mix thoroughly until the ingredients bind together. Divide the mixture into eight equal portions, roll each into a ball and flatten into burger shapes. Roll the burgers in oatbran to cover them completely, put on a plate, cover with cling film and chill.

Brush the burgers on both sides with sunflower oil and place on an oiled baking sheet on the barbecue grill. Cook for 15-20 minutes, turning once.

Spicy mushroom and pecan burgers *Makes 8*

6oz/175g mushrooms, wiped and finely chopped

2oz/50g pecans, grated

2oz/50g fresh wholemeal breadcrumbs

1/2 oz/15g soya flour

2 fl.oz/50ml soya milk

1 onion, peeled and grated

1 garlic clove, crushed

1 dessertspoon sunflower oil

1 rounded teaspoon ground coriander

1 rounded teaspoon ground cumin

1/2 teaspoon turmeric

black pepper

sesame seeds

extra sunflower oil

Heat the dessertspoonful of oil in a pan and gently fry the onion and garlic until soft. Add the ground coriander, cumin and turmeric and stir around for 30 seconds, then remove from the heat and add the mushrooms, pecans and breadcrumbs. Mix the flour with the milk until smooth and add to the other ingredients. Season with black pepper and stir well until the mixture binds together. Divide into eight equal portions, roll each portion into a ball and flatten into burger shapes. Roll the burgers in sesame seeds until covered. Transfer to a plate, cover with cling film and put in the fridge.

Brush the burgers on both sides with sunflower oil and place on an oiled baking sheet on the grill. Cook for 15-20 minutes, turning once.

Carrot and sunflower sausages *Makes 8*

8oz/225g carrot, scraped and grated

2oz/50g sunflower seeds, ground

2oz/50g fresh wholemeal breadcrumbs

$1/2$ oz/15g soya flour

1 onion, peeled and grated

4 tablespoons soya milk

1 rounded tablespoon sunflower spread

1 rounded teaspoon chervil

1 teaspoon paprika

1 teaspoon soy sauce

black pepper

sesame seeds

sunflower oil

Put the carrot, ground sunflower seeds, breadcrumbs, onion, chervil and paprika in a bowl, season with black pepper and stir well. Mix the flour with the milk, sunflower spread and soy sauce until smooth. Add to the carrot mixture and combine thoroughly until it binds. Divide the mixture into eight equal portions. Shape each portion into a sausage, then roll in sesame seeds to cover completely. Put them on a plate, cover and keep in the fridge for a few hours.

Brush the sausages all over with sunflower oil and cook for 15-20 minutes on an oiled baking sheet on the barbecue grill, turning to ensure even cooking.

Nutty sausages   *Makes approx. 15*

4oz/100g carrot, scraped and grated

2oz/50g walnuts, grated

2oz/50g ground almonds

2oz/50g fresh wholemeal breadcrumbs

2oz/50g soya flour

1oz/25g fine wholemeal flour

1 onion, peeled and grated

1 garlic clove, crushed

4 fl.oz/125ml water

1 tablespoon sunflower oil

1 dessertspoon soy sauce

1 rounded teaspoon mixed herbs

1 rounded teaspoon parsley

black pepper

extra sunflower oil

Heat the oil in a saucepan and gently fry the carrot, onion and garlic. Add the wholemeal flour, water and soy sauce, bring to the boil whilst stirring and continue stirring until the sauce thickens. Remove from the heat and add the remaining ingredients. Mix thoroughly until the mixture binds together. Take rounded dessertspoonfuls and roll into small sausage shapes. Put on a plate, cover and refrigerate for a few hours.

Brush the sausages with sunflower oil and cook them on an oiled baking sheet on the grill for 15-20 minutes, turning occasionally.

Mushroom and pine kernel sausages *Makes 9*

4oz/100g mushrooms, wiped and finely chopped

2oz/50g pine kernels, crushed

2oz/50g fresh wholemeal breadcrumbs

2oz/50g fine wholemeal flour

1 onion, peeled and grated

1 garlic clove, crushed

1 dessertspoon olive oil

1 tablespoon soya milk

1 teaspoon parsley

black pepper

sesame seeds

sunflower oil

Heat the oil in a saucepan and fry the onion and garlic until soft. Add the mushrooms and fry for 1 minute, then remove from the heat and stir in the crushed pine kernels, breadcrumbs, flour and parsley. Season with black pepper, add the soya milk and combine thoroughly until the mixture binds. Take heaped dessertspoonfuls of the mixture and form into sausage shapes. Roll each sausage in sesame seeds, put on a plate, cover and keep in the fridge.

Brush the sausages with sunflower oil and place on an oiled baking sheet on the barbecue. Cook for 15-20 minutes, turning regularly.

Peanut and potato patties *Makes 6*

10oz/300g potato, peeled and diced

2oz/50g shelled peanuts, ground

2oz/50g fresh wholemeal breadcrumbs

1oz/25g wheatgerm

1 onion, peeled and grated

1 rounded tablespoon crunchy peanut butter

1 rounded teaspoon chervil

$1/2$ teaspoon yeast extreact

$1/4$ teaspoon paprika

black pepper

1oz/25g shelled peanuts, grated

sunflower oil

Boil the potato until done, drain and dry off over a low heat. Mash the potato and add all other ingredients, except the grated peanuts and sunflower oil. Stir thoroughly until a stiff mixture forms. Divide this into six equal portions, roll each into a ball and flatten into oval shapes. Roll the patties in the grated peanuts and put them on a plate. Cover with cling film and refrigerate for a few hours.

Brush the patties with sunflower oil and place them on an oiled baking tray on the barbecue. Cook for 15-20 minutes, turning once.

Smoked tofu and mushroom medallions *Makes 10*

8oz/225g smoked tofu, mashed

8oz/225g mushrooms, wiped and finely chopped

2oz/50g fresh wholemeal breadcrumbs

2oz/50g fine wholemeal flour

1oz/25g soya flour

1 onion, peeled and grated

6 tablespoons water

1 rounded teaspoon parsley

1 teaspoon soy sauce

black pepper

wheatgerm

sunflower oil

Put the tofu, mushrooms, breadcrumbs, wholemeal flour, onion and parsley in a large bowl and season with black pepper. Mix well. Whisk the soya flour with the water and soy sauce until thick and creamy. Add to the mixture and stir very well until it all binds together. Take heaped tablespoonfuls of the mixture and shape into chunky rounds. Roll each medallion in wheatgerm until completely covered, then transfer to a plate, cover and put in the fridge.

Brush the medallions on both sides with sunflower oil and cook for 15-20 minutes on an oiled baking sheet on the grill, turning once.

Potato and onion rösti cakes *Makes 12*

1$^1/_2$ lb/675g potatoes, scraped

1 onion, peeled and grated

1 dessertspoon parsley

black pepper

sunflower oil

Cut the potatoes into large chunks and boil them for 5 minutes. Drain and allow them to cool, then grate into a bowl. Add the onion and parsley and season with black pepper. Mix thoroughly and divide the mixture into twelve equal portions. Form each portion into a flat round shape.

Cook the rösti cakes on an oiled baking sheet on the barbecue for 15 minutes, turning once.

Tofu and vegetable kebabs *Makes 4*

1lb/450g ingredients chosen from:

a selection of plain, smoked or marinated tofu, cut into 1 inch/2.5cm squares

whole cherry tomatoes, button mushrooms and baby sweetcorn

halved or quartered small onions

diced aubergine

thickly sliced courgette

chunks of red, yellow, green and orange peppers

marinade

2 garlic cloves

2 tablespoons medium sherry

2 tablespoons olive oil

1 dessertspoon soy sauce

1 dessertspoon lemon juice

black pepper

garnish

4 bay leaves

4 sprigs of rosemary

Mix all the marinade ingredients together. Put the prepared kebab ingredients in a bowl and pour the marinade over them. Mix well, cover and leave for a couple of hours to allow the flavours to be absorbed, stirring occasionally.

Thread the ingredients onto 4 square skewers with a bay leaf and a sprig of rosemary and brush with any remaining marinade. Place the kebabs on a hot barbecue grill and cook for 10-15 minutes until tender, turning occasionally.

Brazil nut and butter bean balls *Makes approx. 14*

8oz/225g cooked butter beans, mashed

4oz/100g brazil nuts, ground

1oz/25g brazil nuts, grated

1 onion, peeled and grated

1 rounded tablespoon mixed nut butter

1 tablespoon sunflower oil

1 teaspoon parsley

1 teaspoon soy sauce

1/4 teaspoon paprika

black pepper

extra sunflower oil

Heat the tablespoonful of oil in a saucepan and gently fry the onion. Remove from the heat and add the mashed butter beans, ground brazil nuts, nut butter, parsley, soy sauce and paprika. Season with black pepper and mix thoroughly. Take rounded dessertspoonfuls of the mixture and form into balls. Roll the balls in the grated brazil nuts until completely covered. Put on a plate, cover and refrigerate for a couple of hours.

Brush the balls with sunflower oil and place them on an oiled baking sheet on the barbecue. Cook for 20-25 minutes, turning to ensure even cooking.

Curried bulgar-filled peppers *Serves 4*

4 peppers (each weighing approx. 7oz/200g)

filling

4oz/100g carrot, scraped and grated

4oz/100g cooked sweetcorn kernels

2oz/50g sultanas

2oz/50g bulgar wheat

5 fl.oz/150ml boiling water

1 onion, peeled and finely chopped

2 garlic cloves, crushed

2 tablespoons vegetable oil

2 dessertspoons curry paste

4 cardamoms, husked and the seeds separated

black pepper

Slice the tops off the peppers and remove the seeds and membrane. Blanch the peppers (including the tops) for 2 minutes in boiling water, drain and dry on kitchen paper.

Dissolve the curry paste in the boiling water, add the bulgar wheat and stir well. Leave for 15 minutes until the liquid has been absorbed. Heat the oil in a saucepan and fry the onion and garlic until softened, then add the carrot and stir around for 1 minute. Remove from the heat and add the soaked bulgar wheat together with the remaining ingredients. Combine thoroughly and fill the peppers with this mixture. Put the lids on the peppers and wrap each one in a double layer of kitchen foil. Cook on the barbecue for approximately 30 minutes until tender, turning occasionally.

Almond-stuffed mushrooms *Makes 16*

16 medium-sized cup mushrooms

olive oil

filling

2oz/50g ground almonds

1oz/25g fresh wholemeal breadcrumbs

1oz/25g vegan 'cheddar', grated

2 garlic cloves, crushed

2 tablespoons white wine

1 dessertspoon olive oil

1 rounded teaspoon parsley

black pepper

extra olive oil

Wipe the mushrooms and remove the stalks. Brush the mushrooms all over with olive oil and place them on an oiled baking sheet. Chop the stalks and fry them for a couple of minutes with the garlic in the dessertspoonful of olive oil. Remove from the heat and add the remaining filling ingredients, stirring well until the mixture binds together. Spoon some of this into each mushroom, pressing it down firmly and evenly. Put the baking sheet onto the barbecue grill and cook the mushrooms for 10-15 minutes until just tender.

Jacket potatoes

1 potato per person, each weighing approx. 8-10oz/225-300g

sunflower oil

Wash the potatoes and make a cross on the top of each one with a sharp knife. Brush all over with sunflower oil and wrap individually in kitchen foil. Cook for approximately 1 hour on the barbecue until done, turning occasionally. Serve simply with vegan margarine or grated vegan 'cheese', or top with one of the savoury spreads starting on page 59.

Walnut and mushroom-stuffed tomatoes *Serves 4*

2 large tomatoes (each weighing approx. 12oz/350g)

filling

2oz/50g walnuts, grated

2oz/50g mushrooms, wiped and finely chopped

2oz/50g fresh wholemeal breadcrumbs

1oz/25g vegan 'cheddar', grated

2 garlic cloves, crushed

1 dessertspoon olive oil

1 teaspoon chives

black pepper

vegan 'Parmesan'

Cut the tomatoes in half in a zig-zag pattern. Carefully remove the insides, including the seeds, of the tomatoes and chop finely, put into a sieve and drain off as much liquid as possible. Dry the inside of the tomato shells with kitchen paper.

Heat the oil in a pan and gently fry the mushrooms and garlic for 2 minutes. Add the chopped tomato flesh and cook for a further minute. Remove from the heat and add the remaining filling ingredients except the 'Parmesan'. Combine thoroughly until everything binds together. Carefully fill each of the tomato shells with some of the mixture. Sprinkle 'Parmesan' on top and wrap each tomato half separately in foil. Cook on the barbecue for about 10 minutes.

Cashew and mushroom-stuffed courgettes *Serves 4*

4 courgettes (each weighing approx. 8oz/225g)

filling

3oz/75g mushrooms, wiped and finely chopped

2oz/50g cashew nuts, grated

1 onion, peeled and grated

2 garlic cloves, crushed

1 tablespoon sunflower oil

1 dessertspoon parsley

black pepper

paprika

Cut the courgettes in half lengthwise and scoop out the inside leaving the shells approximately ¼ inch/5mm thick. Finely chop the flesh. Heat the oil in a saucepan and fry the onion and garlic until soft. Add the chopped courgette, mushrooms and parsley and season with black pepper. Cook whilst stirring for 2 minutes. Remove from the heat and add the grated cashews. Mix well, then fill each of the courgette halves with some of the mixture. Sprinkle the tops with paprika and wrap in kitchen foil (two halves to one parcel). Cook on the barbecue for approximately 30 minutes.

Tropical fruit kebabs *Serves 4*

1lb/450g mixed prepared fruits (e.g. pineapple, mango, paw paw,
   banana, star fruit)

3 tablespoons tropical fruit juice

1 tablespoon dark rum

1 dessertspoon golden syrup

1/4 teaspoon ground allspice

Cut the fruit into large chunks and put them in a bowl. Mix the remaining ingredients together and pour over the fruit. Stir well, cover and leave to marinate for 30 minutes. Thread the fruits onto eight small square skewers and cook on the barbecue grill for 5-10 minutes, turning occasionally.

Fruity baked bananas *Serves 4*

4 bananas, peeled

4oz/100g dates, stoned and finely chopped

2oz/50g dried apricots, finely chopped

1 tablespoon medium sherry

4 tablespoons fresh fruit juice

lemon juice

maple syrup

ground cinnamon

Mix the sherry with the fruit juice and add the dates and apricots. Stir well, cover and leave to marinate for 1 hour.

Cut the bananas in half lengthwise, put each banana separately on a double sheet of kitchen foil and sprinkle them with lemon juice. Fill the bananas with some of the marinated fruit mixture and drizzle maple syrup over them. Sprinkle with ground cinnamon and carefully wrap each filled banana. Cook on the barbecue for about 10 minutes.

Spicy baked apples   *Serves 4*

4 cooking apples

6oz/175g mixed cake fruit

1 rounded tablespoon golden syrup

1 rounded teaspoon ground mixed spice

vegan margarine

demerara sugar

Wash the apples and remove the centres with an apple corer. Heat the golden syrup in a saucepan until runny. Remove from the heat and stir in the cake fruit and spice. Fill each apple with some of this mixture, pressing it down firmly. Dot the tops with vegan margarine and sprinkle with demerara sugar. Wrap each apple in a double layer of kitchen foil and cook on the grill for approximately 45 minutes, turning occasionally, until soft.

SAVOURY LOAVES AND PATÉS

S AVOURY LOAVES AND PATÉS ARE IDEAL FOR A BUFFET. THEY CAN BE prepared the day before and kept in the fridge or made well in advance and frozen. They are delicious served cold, but can be served warm if you prefer.

The loaves and patés for slicing are excellent with salads, while the bowls and individual pots of paté can be used for spreading onto bread, rolls and savoury biscuits, or as sandwich fillings.

• *Savoury loaves and patés for slicing* •

Mango, rice and mixed nut paté *Serves 6/8*

6oz/175g mango flesh, finely chopped

4oz/100g long grain brown rice

4oz/100g mixed nuts, ground

4oz/100g fresh wholemeal breadcrumbs

1oz/25g soya flour

1 tablespoon sunflower oil

1 onion, peeled and finely chopped

1 garlic clove, crushed

1 rounded teaspoon ground coriander

$1/2$ teaspoon turmeric

4 cardamoms, husked and the seeds separated

black pepper

Cook the rice, drain and set aside. Heat the oil in a large saucepan and gently fry the onion and garlic until soft. Add the coriander and turmeric and fry for a few seconds more. Remove from the heat and add the cooked rice and remaining ingredients. Mix thoroughly, then spoon into a base-lined and greased 8 inch/20cm loaf tin. Press down firmly and evenly. Cover with foil and bake in a preheated oven at 170°C/325°F/Gas mark 3 for 30 minutes. Run a sharp knife around the edges and carefully invert onto a baking tray. Remove the base lining and return the paté to the oven for 10 minutes until golden. Allow to cool, then put in the fridge until cold. Serve sliced.

Marinated tofu and chickpea bake *Serves 6*

6oz/175g marinated tofu, mashed

6oz/175g cooked chickpeas, mashed

1 onion, peeled and finely chopped

1 garlic clove, crushed

2oz/50g fresh wholemeal breadcrumbs

1 tablespoon sunflower oil

1 rounded tablespoon light tahini

1 teaspoon soy sauce

black pepper

sesame seeds

Heat the oil in a saucepan and fry the onion and garlic until soft. Remove from the heat and add the remaining ingredients except the sesame seeds. Mix thoroughly and spoon the mixture into a lined and greased 7 inch/18cm square flan tin. Press down firmly and evenly and sprinkle the top with sesame seeds. Bake in a preheated oven at 180°C/350°F/Gas mark 4 for approximately 35 minutes until golden brown.

Sunflower and soya loaf *Serves 6/8*

4oz/100g sunflower seeds, ground

2oz/50g natural minced textured vegetable protein

2oz/50g fresh wholemeal breadcrumbs

1/2 oz/15g soya flour

10 fl.oz/300ml boiling water

1 onion, peeled and finely chopped

1 garlic clove, crushed

1 tablespoon sunflower oil

1 teaspoon soy sauce

1 teaspoon mixed herbs

1/2 teaspoon yeast extract

black pepper

Dissolve the yeast extract and soy sauce in the boiling water. Add the textured vegetable protein and leave for 1 hour. Heat the oil in a saucepan and gently fry the onion and garlic. Remove from the heat and add the soaked vegetable protein and remaining ingredients. Mix thoroughly, then spoon the mixture into an 8 inch/20cm base-lined and greased loaf tin. Press down firmly and evenly and cover with foil. Bake in a preheated oven at 180°C/350°F/Gas mark 4 for 35 minutes. Remove the foil and bake for a further 20-25 minutes until golden. Allow to cool in the tin for 15 minutes, then run a sharp knife around the edges and turn the loaf out. Put in the fridge until cold.

Chickpea and hazelnut paté *Serves 6*

8oz/225g cooked chickpeas, mashed

2oz/50g hazelnuts, grated

2oz/50g carrot, scraped and grated

1 onion, peeled and finely chopped

1 rounded tablespoon hazelnut spread or light tahini

2 tablespoons soya milk

1 tablespoon olive oil

1 teaspoon soy sauce

black pepper

flaked hazelnuts

Heat the oil in a large saucepan and gently fry the onion. Remove from the heat and add the chickpeas, grated hazelnuts and carrot. Mix the hazelnut spread or tahini with the soya milk and soy sauce until smooth and add to the mixture in the saucepan. Season with black pepper and combine well. Spoon the mixture into a lined and greased 7 inch/18cm diameter flan tin, pressing it down evenly. Sprinkle the top with flaked hazelnuts and push these in lightly with the back of a spoon. Bake in a preheated oven at 180°C/350°F/Gas mark 4 for about 35 minutes until browned.

Aubergine and brazil nut paté *Serves 6*

12oz/350g aubergine, finely chopped

3oz/75g brazil nuts, grated

2oz/50g fresh wholemeal breadcrumbs

1oz/25g soya flour

1 onion, peeled and finely chopped

2 tablespoons vegetable oil

1 teaspoon soy sauce

$1/2$ teaspoon paprika

black pepper

flaked brazil nuts

Heat the oil in a large saucepan and fry the aubergine and onion for 10 minutes until softened and reduced down, stirring frequently to prevent sticking. Remove from the heat and add all remaining ingredients except the flaked nuts. Mix thoroughly and spoon evenly into a lined and greased 7 inch/18cm diameter flan tin. Level the top and sprinkle with flaked nuts. Bake in a preheated oven at 180°C/350°F/Gas mark 4 for 35-40 minutes until golden brown.

Herby courgette, rice and pecan loaf   *Serves 6/8*

6oz/175g courgette, grated

4oz/100g long grain rice

4oz/100g pecans, grated

2oz/50g fresh wholemeal breadcrumbs

1 onion, peeled and finely chopped

1 garlic clove, crushed

2 dessertspoons olive oil

1oz/25g soya flour

4 tablespoons soya milk

2 rounded teaspoons herbes du Provence

$1/4$ teaspoon ground bay leaves

black pepper

Cook the rice and allow to drain in a sieve for 5 minutes. Heat 1 dessertspoonful of olive oil in a large saucepan and fry the onion and garlic until soft. Remove from the heat and add the rice, courgette, pecans, breadcrumbs, herbes du Provence and ground bay leaves. Season with black pepper and combine well. Mix the soya flour with the other dessertspoonful of olive oil and the soya milk until thick. Add this to the mixture and stir thoroughly. Spoon the mixture into a lined and greased 8 inch/20cm loaf tin, pressing it down firmly and evenly. Cover with foil and bake in a preheated oven at 180°C/350°F/Gas mark 4 for 40 minutes, then remove the foil and bake for a further 15 minutes. Turn out onto a baking tray and carefully peel off the lining paper. Return to the oven for approximately 10 minutes to brown.

• *Bowls of paté* •

Mushroom and sunflower seed paté *Serves 6/8*

6oz/175g mushrooms, wiped and finely chopped

4oz/100g sunflower seeds, ground

2oz/50g natural minced textured vegetable protein

2oz/50g fresh wholemeal breadcrumbs

1 onion, peeled and finely chopped

2 garlic cloves, crushed

1 tablespoon olive oil

2 tablespoons boiling water

5 fl.oz/150ml boiling water

1 rounded tablespoon sunflower spread

1 teaspoon soy sauce

1 teaspoon parsley

1/2 teaspoon yeast extract

black pepper

extra sunflower seeds

Dissolve the yeast extract in the 5 fl.oz/150ml boiling water. Add the textured vegetable protein, stir well and leave for 10 minutes. Heat the oil in a saucepan and gently fry the onion and garlic. Add the mushrooms and fry for a minute or two more until the juices begin to run. Remove from the heat and add the soaked vegetable protein, ground sunflower seeds, breadcrumbs and parsley. Season with black pepper and mix well. Combine the sunflower spread with the soy sauce and 2 tablespoonfuls of boiling water until smooth. Mix thoroughly with the vegetable protein mixture and spoon into a greased 7 inch/18cm diameter ovenproof dish. Press down firmly and evenly. Sprinkle the top with sunflower seeds and push these in lightly with the back of a spoon. Bake in a preheated oven at 180°C/350°F/Gas mark 4 for approximately 35 minutes until golden brown. Serve in the dish, either warm or cold.

Celery, buckwheat and brazil nut paté   *Serves 6/8*

8oz/225g celery, trimmed and finely chopped

4oz/100g roasted buckwheat

3oz/75g brazil nuts

1 onion, peeled and finely chopped

8 fl.oz/225ml water

2 fl.oz 50ml water

1 tablespoon vegetable oil

1 teaspoon soy sauce

1 rounded teaspoon parsley

black pepper

Put the buckwheat, 8 fl.oz/225ml water and soy sauce into a small saucepan and bring to the boil, cover and simmer very gently until the liquid has been absorbed. Stir frequently to prevent sticking.

Heat the oil in a saucepan and gently fry the celery and onion for 10 minutes. Add the 2 fl.oz/50ml water and bring to the boil, cover and simmer for 5 minutes. Remove from the heat and blend. Add the cooked buckwheat and mix well. Flake three of the brazil nuts and reserve for garnishing, grate the rest and add to the celery and buckwheat mixture. Add the parsley and season with black pepper. Mix thoroughly, then spoon the mixture into a greased 7 inch/18cm diameter ovenproof dish. Sprinkle the flaked brazil nuts on top and press these in lightly with the back of a spoon. Bake in a preheated oven at 180°C/350°F/Gas mark 4 for 35 minutes until browned.

Aubergine and pine kernel paté *Serves 6/8*

1lb/450g aubergine, finely chopped

3oz/75g pine kernels, grated

2oz/50g fresh wholemeal breadcrumbs

1 onion, peeled and finely chopped

2 garlic cloves, crushed

2 tablespoons olive oil

1 teaspoon balsamic vinegar

$1/2$ teaspoon thyme

black pepper

extra pine kernels

Heat the oil in a large saucepan and fry the aubergine, onion and garlic for
12-15 minutes until reduced down and soft. Stir frequently to prevent
sticking. Remove from the heat and add the remaining ingredients, except the
extra pine kernels. Mix thoroughly and spoon the mixture into a greased 7
inch/18cm diameter ovenproof dish. Push it down firmly and evenly and
sprinkle with pine kernels, pressing them in lightly with the back of a spoon.
Bake in a preheated oven at 180°C/350°F/Gas mark 4 for about 35 minutes
until golden.

Curried carrot, millet and almond paté *Serves 6/8*

8oz/225g carrot, scraped and grated

4oz/100g millet

2oz/50g ground almonds

1oz/25g dried dates, finely chopped

1 onion, peeled and finely chopped

10 fl.oz/300ml water

1 tablespoon sunflower oil

1 rounded teaspoon curry powder

1/2 teaspoon ground cumin

1/2 teaspoon paprika

4 cardamom pods, husked and the seeds separated

black pepper

chopped flaked almonds

Heat the oil in a saucepan and gently fry the carrot and onion for 3 minutes. Add the curry powder, cumin, paprika and cardamom seeds and stir around for a few seconds. Add the millet, dates and water and stir well. Bring to the boil, cover and simmer gently until the liquid has been absorbed, stirring frequently and removing the lid towards the end of cooking. Take off the heat and add the ground almonds, season with black pepper and mix thoroughly. Spoon the mixture into a greased 7 inch/18cm ovenproof dish and press it down firmly and evenly. Sprinkle the top with chopped flaked almonds and push these in lightly. Bake in a preheated oven at 180°C/350°F/Gas mark 4 for approximately 30 minutes.

• *Individual paté pots* •

The following are all baked in individual ramekin dishes of approximately 2½ inches/6cm diameter. They are served in the dishes, either warm or cold.

Smoked tofu and brazil nut paté *Makes 6*

9oz/250g smoked tofu, grated

3oz/75g brazil nuts, grated

2oz/50g fresh wholemeal breadcrumbs

1 onion, peeled and finely chopped

1 tablespoon sunflower oil

½oz/15g soya flour

2 rounded tablespoons light tahini

3 fl.oz/75ml water

1 teaspoon soy sauce

black pepper

Heat the oil in a large saucepan and fry the onion until softened. Remove from the heat and add the tofu, brazil nuts and breadcrumbs. Mix the soya flour with the tahini, water and soy sauce until smooth, then add to the mixture. Season with black pepper and stir thoroughly. Divide between six greased ramekin dishes, pressing the mixture in firmly and evenly. Bake in a preheated oven at 180°C/350°F/Gas mark 4 for approximately 30 minutes until golden.

Spiced chickpea and walnut paté *Makes 6*

12oz/350g cooked chickpeas, mashed

4oz/100g carrot, scraped and grated

2oz/50g walnuts, grated

1 onion, peeled and finely chopped

2 rounded tablespoons light tahini

1 tablespoon sunflower oil

1 teaspoon ground coriander

1 teaspoon ground cumin

1/2 teaspoon paprika

black pepper

6 walnut halves

Heat the oil in a large saucepan and gently fry the onion. Add the carrot and stir around for 1 minute. Stir in the coriander, cumin and paprika, then remove from the heat and add the chickpeas, grated walnuts and tahini. Season with black pepper and mix thoroughly. Divide the mixture between six greased dishes, pressing down firmly and evenly. Place a walnut half on top of each one and bake in a preheated oven at 180°C/350°F/Gas mark 4 for about 30 minutes.

Mushroom, lentil and cranberry paté *Makes 6*

6oz/175g mushrooms, wiped and finely chopped

4oz/100g puy lentils

2oz/50g cranberry sauce

1$^1/_2$ oz/40g fresh wholemeal breadcrumbs

1oz/25g soya flour

1 onion, peeled and finely chopped

1 garlic clove, crushed

1 dessertspoon sunflower oil

1 teaspoon soy sauce

$^1/_2$ teaspoon ground coriander

black pepper

Cook the lentils until tender, drain thoroughly and mash with a potato masher. Heat the oil in a large saucepan and fry the onion and garlic. Add the mushrooms and fry for a further 2 minutes. Remove from the heat, add the lentils and remaining ingredients and combine well. Divide between six greased dishes and press the mixture down firmly and evenly. Bake in a preheated oven at 180°C/350°F/Gas mark 4 for approximately 35 minutes until golden brown.

Spicy chestnut, apple and hazelnut paté *Makes 6*

8oz/225g peeled chestnuts, grated

8oz/225g cooking apple, peeled, cored and grated

2oz/50g hazelnuts, grated

2oz/50g sultanas, chopped

1 onion, peeled and finely chopped

1 rounded tablespoon hazelnut butter

1 tablespoon sunflower oil

1 teaspoon ground coriander

1 teaspoon ground cumin

1/4 teaspoon ground cinnamon

black pepper

Heat the oil in a large saucepan and fry the onion until softened. Add the coriander, cumin, cinnamon and chestnuts and stir around for 1 minute more. Remove from the heat and add the remaining ingredients, mixing well, then divide between six greased ramekin dishes, pressing down firmly. Bake in a preheated oven at 180°C/350°F/Gas mark 4 for 35 minutes or so until golden.

PASTRIES

Pastries come in all shapes and sizes — from the ever-popular flans to little individual bites and larger pies and strudels which can be sliced. Luckily most shop-bought puff and filo pastry is suitable for vegans, which is very convenient as these two types of pastry are quite time-consuming to make.

All the pastries here can be frozen and may be served either hot or cold.

Savoury palmiers *Makes 12*

9oz/250g puff pastry
vegan 'Parmesan' substitute

filling
2oz/50g mushrooms, wiped and finely chopped
2oz/50g red pepper, finely chopped
2oz/50g green pepper, finely chopped
2oz/50g fresh wholemeal breadcrumbs
2oz/50g vegan 'cheese', grated
1 garlic clove, crushed
1 rounded dessertspoon tomato purée
1 dessertspoon olive oil
1 rounded teaspoon herbes du Provence
black pepper

Heat the oil in a saucepan and gently fry the mushrooms, red and green pepper and garlic for 1 minute. Remove from the heat, add the breadcrumbs, grated 'cheese', tomato purée and herbes du Provence, season with black pepper and mix thoroughly.

Roll out the pastry to an oblong measuring 11 x 9 inches/28 x 23cm. Spread the filling evenly over the pastry. Roll the two long sides towards the centre and enclose the filling. Dampen the edges with water and pinch together to join. Cut the roll into twelve equal slices. Grease and lightly flour a baking tray. Place the slices flat on the tray and sprinkle them with 'Parmesan' substitute. Bake in a preheated oven at 170°C/325°F/Gas mark 3 for about 45 minutes until golden brown.

Curried chestnut and mushroom parcels *Makes 8*

9oz/250g puff pastry

soya milk

sesame seeds

filling

8oz/225g shelled chestnuts, grated

6oz/175g mushrooms, wiped and finely chopped

1 onion, peeled and finely chopped

1/2 oz/15g soya flour

3 tablespoons water

1 tablespoon vegetable oil

1 dessertspoon curry paste

black pepper

Heat the oil in a saucepan and fry the onion until soft. Add the mushrooms and cook until the juices begin to run. Add the chestnuts and stir around for a few seconds, then remove from the heat. Mix the soya flour with the water and curry paste until smooth. Add to the chestnut mixture and season with black pepper. Stir well and set aside.

Cut the pastry into eight equal pieces and roll out each piece on a floured board to a 5½ inch/14cm square. Divide the filling between the squares.

Dampen the pastry edges with soya milk, bring the four corners over to the middle to enclose the filling and pinch the edges together to join. Make 4 slits in the top of each parcel with a sharp knife, brush the tops with soya milk and sprinkle with sesame seeds. Transfer to a greased baking sheet and bake in a preheated oven at 170°C/325°F/Gas mark 3 for approximately 35 minutes until browned.

Buffet pie *Serves 6*

9oz/250g puff pastry

soya milk

sesame seeds

filling

3oz/75g shelled chestnuts, grated

3oz/75g mixed nuts, grated

3oz/75g mushrooms, wiped and finely chopped

3oz/75g carrot, scraped and grated

1oz/25g sunflower seeds

1oz/25g raisins

1 eating apple, peeled, cored and grated

1 onion, peeled and finely chopped

1 celery stick, trimmed and finely chopped

2 garlic cloves, crushed

1 rounded tablespoon light tahini

1 tablespoon sunflower oil

1 teaspoon soy sauce

1 teaspoon parsley

1/2 teaspoon paprika

black pepper

Heat the oil in a saucepan and gently fry the onion, celery and garlic. Add the carrot and mushrooms and fry for another minute. Remove from the heat and add the remaining filling ingredients. Mix thoroughly and set aside.

Take two-thirds of the pastry and roll out to fit a greased loose-bottomed 8 inch/20cm diameter flan tin. Spoon the filling into the flan case and press it down firmly and evenly. Roll out the remaining pastry into a circle to fit the top. Press the edges together using a fork, then prick the top all over. Brush with soya milk and sprinkle with sesame seeds. Bake in a preheated oven at 170°C/325°F/Gas mark 3 for 35 minutes or so until golden.

Mixed nut and seed pasties *Makes 8*

9oz/250g puff pastry

soya milk

black onion seeds

filling

4oz/100g mixed nuts, ground

3oz/75g carrot, peeled and grated

3oz/75g fresh wholemeal breadcrumbs

1oz/25g sunflower seeds

1oz/25g linseed

1oz/25g sesame seeds

1oz/25g soya flour

1 onion, peeled and finely chopped

1 garlic clove, crushed

2 tablespoon sunflower oil

1 rounded tablespoons sunflower spread

1 dessertspoon soy sauce

1 rounded teaspoon chervil

1 rounded teaspoon thyme

black pepper

4 fl.oz/125ml soya milk

Heat the oil in a large saucepan and fry the onion, garlic and carrot for 2 minutes. Remove from the heat and add the mixed nuts, breadcrumbs, sunflower seeds, linseed, sesame seeds, chervil and thyme. Season with black pepper and stir well. Mix the sunflower spread with the soya flour, soya milk and soy sauce until smooth. Add to the mixture and combine thoroughly.

Cut the puff pastry into eight equal portions. Roll each portion into a ball, then roll out into a 6½ inch/16.5cm circle. Divide the filling between the pastry circles, placing it neatly in the middle. Brush the edges of the pastry with water and pinch together enclosing the filling. Make three slits on each side of the pasties with a sharp knife, brush with soya milk and sprinkle with black onion seeds. Carefully transfer to a greased baking tray and bake in a preheated oven at 170°C/325°F/Gas mark 3 for approximately 35 minutes.

Sunflower seed and carrot patties *Makes 12*

12oz/350g fine wholemeal self raising flour
4oz/100g vegan margarine, melted
¼ oz/7g sachet easy-blend yeast
approx. 6 fl.oz./175ml soya milk, warmed
wheatgerm
extra soya milk
sunflower seeds

filling
1lb/450g carrots, scraped and grated
6oz/175g sunflower seeds, ground
1 onion, peeled and finely chopped
2 garlic cloves, crushed
2 tablespoons sunflower oil
1 dessertspoon soy sauce
1 teaspoon paprika
black pepper

Mix the flour and yeast, stir in the melted margarine and gradually add enough warmed soya milk for the mixture to bind. Knead well, then return to the bowl, cover and leave in a warm place for 1 hour.

Heat the oil in a large saucepan and gently fry the carrot, onion and garlic for 5 minutes, stirring frequently. Remove from the heat and add the remaining filling ingredients.

Knead the pastry again and divide it into twelve equal portions. Sprinkle some wheatgerm on the board and roll out each piece of dough into a 6 inch/15cm diameter circle. Divide the filling between the circles, placing it neatly in the centre. Fold the pastry edges towards the centre to enclose the filling and make a round shape. Place the rounds on a greased baking sheet with the joins underneath and make 3 slits in the top of each patty with a sharp knife. Brush with soya milk and sprinkle some sunflower seeds on each one. Bake in a preheated oven at 180°C/350°F/Gas mark 4 for 25-30 minutes until golden.

Creamy sweetcorn and pistachio tarts *Makes 12*

pastry
9oz/250g fine wholemeal self raising flour

4oz/100g vegan margarine

water

chopped pistachio nuts

filling
4oz/100g frozen sweetcorn kernels

2oz/50g frozen sweetcorn kernels, thawed

2oz/50g pistachios, ground

1 onion, peeled and chopped

2 fl.oz/50ml water

5 fl.oz/150ml soya milk

1 rounded tablespoon cornflour

1 tablespoon olive oil

1 teaspoon balsamic vinegar

$^1/_2$ teaspoon thyme

black pepper

Rub the margarine into the flour and add enough water to bind. Turn out onto a floured board and knead. Divide the dough into twelve equal portions. Roll each portion into a ball, then roll it out into a 4½ inches/11cm diameter round. Line a 12-holed greased muffin tin with the pastry circles. Prick the bases and bake blind in a preheated oven at 170°C/325°F/Gas mark 3 for 5 minutes.

Heat the oil in a saucepan and fry the onion until soft. Add the 4oz/100g sweetcorn, water, balsamic vinegar and thyme and bring to the boil. Cover and simmer gently for 5 minutes. Transfer to a blender and blend until smooth. Return to the saucepan, bring to the boil whilst stirring and continue stirring until the sauce thickens. Remove from the heat and stir in the ground pistachios and thawed sweetcorn. Season with black pepper and mix well. Divide this mixture between the pastry cases and sprinkle with chopped pistachio nuts. Return to the oven for about 15 minutes until browned. Allow to cool in the tin.

Peanut samosas   *Makes 8*

8oz/225g fine wholemeal self raising flour

2¹/₂ oz/40g vegan margarine

1 teaspoon paprika

soya milk

sunflower oil

black onion seeds

filling

2oz/50g frozen peas, thawed

2oz/50g cooked black-eye beans

1oz/25g natural minced textured vegetable protein

1oz/25g sultanas

1 onion, peeled and grated

2 garlic cloves, crushed

4 fl.oz/125ml boiling water

1 rounded tablespoon peanut butter

1 tablespoon sunflower oil

1 teaspoon black mustard seeds

1 rounded teaspoon ground coriander

1 rounded teaspoon ground cumin

$1/2$ teaspoon turmeric

$1/2$ teaspoon yeast extract

3 cardamoms, husked and the seeds separated

black pepper

Dissolve the yeast extract in the boiling water. Add the textured vegetable protein, stir and leave for 30 minutes. Heat the oil in a saucepan and fry the onion and garlic until softened. Add the mustard and cardamom seeds, coriander, cumin and turmeric and stir around for 1 minute. Remove from the heat and add the soaked vegetable protein, peas, black-eye beans, sultanas and peanut butter. Season with black pepper and mix very well.

Mix the paprika with the flour and rub in the margarine. Add enough soya milk to form a soft dough. Turn out onto a floured board and knead well. Divide the dough into eight equal portions. Roll each portion into a ball, then roll these out into circles of about 4½ inches/11cm diameter.

Divide the filling between the pastry circles. Dampen the edges with soya milk and fold them over to enclose the filling. Press the edges together with a fork. Carefully transfer the samosas to a greased baking sheet. Prick the tops with a fork and brush with sunflower oil. Sprinkle with black onion seeds and bake in a preheated oven at 180°C/350°F/Gas mark 4 for approximately 15 minutes until golden.

Spinach and potato roll-ups *Makes 16*

8oz/225g fine wholemeal self raising flour

2oz/50g vegan margarine

1 teaspoon paprika

soya milk

filling

10oz/300g potato, scraped

2oz/50g frozen, cooked, finely chopped spinach, thawed

2oz/50g vegan 'cheddar', grated

1 onion, peeled and grated

1 tablespoon olive oil

$1/2$ teaspoon marjoram

pinch of grated nutmeg

black pepper

Cut the potato into even-sized chunks and boil for 10 minutes. Drain and allow to cool, then grate. Heat the oil in a saucepan and gently fry the onion. Remove from the heat and add the grated potato and remaining filling ingredients. Mix thoroughly and set aside.

Mix the paprika with the flour and rub in the margarine. Add soya milk until a soft dough forms. Turn out onto a floured piece of cling film and roll out to an oblong shape of 12 x 9 inches/30 x 23cm. Spread the filling evenly over the pastry, leaving a 1 inch/2.5cm gap along one of the long edges. Dampen this exposed edge with soya milk. Starting from the other long edge, carefully roll up the oblong to enclose the filling (pulling up the cling film helps to get this started). Cut the roll into sixteen equal slices with a sharp knife. Put the slices flat on a greased baking sheet and bake in a preheated oven at 180°C/350°F/Gas mark 4 for 25-30 minutes until golden brown.

Asparagus, rice and walnut strudel   *Serves 8*

9¹/₂ oz/270g packet of filo pastry

olive oil

sesame seeds

filling

1lb/450g asparagus, trimmed

8oz/225g vegan 'cream cheese'

4oz/100g arborio rice

2oz/50g walnuts, finely chopped

1 onion, peeled and finely chopped

2 garlic cloves, crushed

1 dessertspoon olive oil

2 fl.oz/50ml white wine

10 fl.oz/300ml water

1 rounded teaspoon marjoram

¹/₂ teaspoon yeast extract

¹/₄ teaspoon ground bay leaves

black pepper

Heat the dessertspoonful of olive oil in a saucepan and fry the onion and garlic until soft. Add the rice and fry for a further minute. Add the wine, water, yeast extract, marjoram and ground bay leaves and stir well. Bring to the boil, cover and simmer until the liquid has been absorbed and the rice is cooked. Cut the asparagus into ¹/₂ inch/1cm lengths and steam until tender. Add to the rice together with the remaining filling ingredients. Mix well and set aside.

Place one-third of the filo sheets on a flat surface, lightly brushing between each sheet with olive oil. Spread half the filling mixture evenly along the centre of the sheets, leaving a gap of a couple of inches on all sides for folding over. Repeat these layers and finish with a layer of filo pastry. Fold the four pastry edges in towards the centre, then carefully transfer the strudel with the join underneath to a greased baking sheet. Brush the top all over with olive oil and sprinkle with sesame seeds. Cover with foil and bake in a preheated oven at 180°C/350°F/Gas mark 4 for 20 minutes. Remove the foil and bake for a further 20-25 minutes until golden. Cut into slices.

• *Savoury flans* •

The following fillings are for an 8 inch/20cm diameter pastry flan case. The flans can be served either hot or cold.

Pastry flan case

> 6oz/175g fine wholemeal self raising flour
> 2¹/₂ oz/60g vegan margarine
> water

Rub the margarine into the flour and add enough cold water to bind. Turn out onto a floured board and roll out to fit a greased 8 inch/20cm diameter loose-bottomed flan tin. Prick the base with a fork and bake blind in a preheated oven at 180°C/350°F/Gas mark 4 for 5 minutes.

Chestnut and mushroom flan *Serves 6*

> 8oz/225g shelled chestnuts, grated
> 4oz/100g mushrooms, wiped and finely chopped
> 1 onion, peeled and finely chopped
> 1 garlic clove, crushed
> 1 tablespoon vegetable oil
> 1 dessertspoon soy sauce
> 1 rounded teaspoon ground coriander
> black pepper
> 3 fl.oz/75ml soya milk
> ¹/₂ oz/15g soya flour

Heat the oil in a saucepan and gently fry the onion and garlic. Add the mushrooms and ground coriander and fry for a further minute, then remove from the heat and stir in the grated chestnuts. Mix the soya flour with the soya milk and soy sauce until smooth, add to the pan and season with black pepper. Mix thoroughly and spoon into the pastry case, pressing down firmly. Bake in a preheated oven at 180°C/350°F/Gas mark 4 for 30 minutes until golden brown.

Smoked tofu and almond flan *Serves 6*

8oz/225g smoked tofu, mashed

4oz/100g almonds, grated

1 onion, peeled and finely chopped

6 tablespoons soya milk

1 rounded tablespoon light tahini

1 tablespoon sunflower oil

1 teaspoon soy sauce

1 teaspoon parsley

black pepper

flaked almonds

Heat the oil in a saucepan and gently fry the onion. Remove from the heat and add the tofu, grated almonds and parsley. Mix the tahini with the soya milk and soy sauce until smooth. Add this to the mixture and season with black pepper. Combine well and spoon the mixture evenly into an 8 inch/20cm pastry case. Level the top and sprinkle with flaked almonds, pressing them in lightly with the back of a spoon. Bake the flan for 30-35 minutes at 180°C/350°F/Gas mark 4.

Aubergine and hazelnut flan *Serves 6*

9oz/250g aubergine, finely chopped

2oz/50g hazelnuts, grated

2oz/50g fresh wholemeal breadcrumbs

$1/2$ oz/15g soya flour

1 onion, peeled and finely chopped

2 tablespoons sunflower oil

3 tablespoons soya milk

1 rounded tablespoon hazelnut butter

1 rounded teaspoon chervil

$1/2$ teaspoon soy sauce

$1/4$ teaspoon celery seed

black pepper

$1/2$ oz/15g hazelnuts, flaked

Heat the oil in a saucepan and gently fry the aubergine and onion for 10 minutes, stirring frequently to prevent sticking. Remove from the heat and add the grated hazelnuts, breadcrumbs, chervil and celery seed. Season with black pepper and stir well. Blend the hazelnut butter with the soy sauce, soya milk and soya flour until smooth. Add to the mixture and combine thoroughly. Spoon the mixture into an 8 inch/20cm pastry case and sprinkle the flaked hazelnuts on top. Press these in lightly with the back of a spoon. Bake in a preheated oven at 180°C/350°F/Gas mark 4 for 30-35 minutes until golden.

Savoury bulgar and nut flan *Serves 6*

2oz/50g bulgar wheat

2oz/50g mixed nuts, grated

2oz/50g mushrooms

2oz/50g red pepper

2oz/50g green pepper

2oz/50g yellow pepper

1 onion, peeled and finely chopped

1 garlic clove, crushed

4 fl.oz/125ml boiling water

1 tablespoon sunflower oil

1 rounded tablespoon mixed nut butter

$1/2$ teaspoon paprika

$1/2$ teaspoon yeast extract

$1/4$ teaspoon celery seed

black pepper

sunflower seeds

Dissolve the yeast extract in the boiling water. Add the bulgar wheat, cover and leave for 30 minutes. Finely chop the red, green and yellow peppers and the mushrooms. Heat the oil in a large saucepan and gently fry the peppers, onion and garlic until soft. Add the mushrooms and stir around for a few seconds. Remove from the heat. Drain the bulgar wheat in a fine sieve and press out any excess water. Add the bulgar to the pan together with all remaining ingredients except the sunflower seeds. Mix thoroughly and spoon evenly into an 8 inch/20cm pastry case. Press the mixture down firmly and sprinkle with sunflower seeds, pressing these in lightly with the back of a spoon. Bake the flan in a preheated oven at 180°C/350°F/Gas mark 4 for about 35 minutes until golden brown.

Curried parsnip, banana and brazil nut flan *Serves 6*

12oz/350g parsnip, peeled and grated

1 small banana (approx. 4oz/100g), peeled and mashed

2oz/50g brazil nuts, grated

1 onion, peeled and finely chopped

2 tablespoons sunflower oil

1 rounded teaspoon curry powder

$1/2$ teaspoon ground coriander

$1/4$ teaspoon turmeric

black pepper

4 brazil nuts, flaked

Heat the oil in a large saucepan and gently fry the parsnip, onion, curry powder, ground coriander and turmeric for 5 minutes, stirring frequently. Remove from the heat and stir in the grated brazil nuts and banana; season with black pepper and mix well. Spoon the mixture into an 8 inch/20cm pastry flan case and press it down evenly. Sprinkle the flaked brazil nuts on top and push these in lightly with the back of a spoon. Bake in a preheated oven at 180°C/350°F/Gas mark 4 for approximately 35 minutes.

Asparagus and pumpkin seed flan *Serves 6*

12oz/350g asparagus, trimmed

1 onion, peeled and finely chopped

4 fl.oz/125ml water

4 fl.oz/125ml soya milk

2oz/50g pumpkin seeds, ground

2oz/50g fresh wholemeal breadcrumbs

1 rounded tablespoon cornflour

1 tablespoon olive oil

1/4 teaspoon celery seed

1/4 teaspoon yeast extract

1/2 teaspoon thyme

black pepper

extra pumpkin seeds

Cut the top 2 inches/5cm of tip from each asparagus stalk and set aside. Finely chop the remaining stalks and fry with the onion in the olive oil for 5 minutes. Add the water, celery seed, yeast extract and thyme and season with black pepper. Bring to the boil, cover and simmer for about 10 minutes until tender. Transfer to a liquidiser with half the soya milk. Blend until smooth then return to the saucepan. Mix the cornflour with the remaining soya milk until smooth, and add to the purée. Stir well. Bring to the boil whilst stirring for a few seconds until the mixture thickens. Remove from the heat and add the breadcrumbs and ground pumpkin seeds. Steam the asparagus tips until just tender, cut them into 1/2 inch/1cm lengths and add to the mixture. Spoon the filling evenly into the pastry case and sprinkle the top with pumpkin seeds. Bake in a preheated oven at 180°C/350°F/Gas mark 4 for approximately 30 minutes more.

SALADS

Not only do salads look good, they are also packed with vitamins and minerals, as vegetables, fruits, nuts, beans, pulses, pasta and grains can all be made into salads. Most are very easy to prepare and can be served with main courses and buffet meals at any time of the year. Choose the freshest ingredients available and prepare salads no more than a couple of hours before required.

Pineapple and pistachio rice salad *Serves 4*

4oz/100g long grain brown rice

4oz/100g peeled fresh pineapple, finely chopped

1oz/25g pistachios, chopped

2 spring onions, trimmed and finely sliced

1 dessertspoon sunflower oil

10 fl.oz/300ml water

$1/4$ teaspoon turmeric

1 teaspoon chervil

black pepper

chopped fresh parsley

Heat the oil in a saucepan and gently fry the spring onions and rice for 2 minutes. Add the turmeric, chervil and water and season with black pepper. Stir well and bring to the boil, cover and simmer gently until the liquid has been absorbed and the rice is cooked. Put in a lidded container and refrigerate until cold. Fork through the rice and add the pineapple and pistachios. Mix well and transfer to a serving dish. Garnish with chopped fresh parsley.

Fruity brown rice and lentil salad *Serves 4*

2oz/50g long grain brown rice

2oz/50g brown lentils

1 small onion, peeled and grated

1/4 oz/7g root ginger, peeled and finely chopped

4 dried dates, finely chopped

4 dried apricots, finely chopped

1 tablespoon sultanas

1 tablespoon raisins

1 dessertspoon vegetable oil

1 cardamom, husked and the seeds separated

1/2 teaspoon coriander seeds

1/4 teaspoon ground cloves

10 fl.oz./300ml water

2 fl.oz./50ml fresh orange juice

Soak the lentils in water for 2 hours, drain and put them in a fresh pan of water. Boil for 10 minutes, drain again and set aside.

Heat the oil in a saucepan and fry the onion and ginger until softened. Add the rice and lentils and stir around for 1 minute. Add the remaining ingredients and combine well. Bring to the boil, cover and simmer gently for about 30 minutes until the liquid has been absorbed and the mixture is thick. Transfer to a covered container and chill before serving.

Saffron, millet and pepper salad *Serves 4*

4oz/100g millet

2oz/50g red pepper, finely chopped

2oz/50g yellow pepper, finely chopped

2oz/50g green pepper, finely chopped

1 onion, peeled and finely chopped

1 dessertspoon sunflower oil

10 fl.oz./300ml water

few strands of saffron

black pepper

1/2oz/15g pumpkin seeds

chopped fresh chives

1 tomato, cut into wedges

Heat the oil in a saucepan and gently fry the onion. Add the millet and fry for 1 minute more. Add the peppers, water and saffron, season with black pepper and stir well. Bring to the boil, cover and simmer for about 20 minutes until the liquid has been absorbed and the millet is done. Put in a lidded container in the fridge until cold. Fork through the salad and stir in the pumpkin seeds. Transfer to a serving dish and garnish with chopped fresh chives and tomato wedges.

Multicoloured pasta salad *Serves 4*

2oz/50g tiny pasta shells

2oz/50g frozen peas

2oz/50g frozen sweetcorn kernels

2oz/50g cauliflower, cut into tiny florets

2oz/50g red pepper, finely chopped

2oz/50g orange pepper, finely chopped

2oz/50g black grapes, seeded and quartered

1 dessertspoon olive oil

1 tablespoon white wine vinegar

1 teaspoon parsley

black pepper

Cook the pasta, drain and rinse under cold running water. Drain well and put in a bowl with the red and orange peppers and the grapes. Steam the peas, sweetcorn and cauliflower until just tender. Rinse under cold running water, drain well and add to the pasta. Mix the olive oil with the vinegar and pour over the salad. Add the parsley and season with black pepper. Toss well and transfer to a serving bowl. Cover and put in the fridge before serving.

Butter bean, wild rice and sunflower seed salad

Serves 6

> 8oz/225g cooked butter beans
>
> 4oz/100g wild and long grain brown rice mix
>
> 2oz/50g carrot, scraped and grated
>
> 1oz/25g sunflower seeds, toasted
>
> 2 spring onions, trimmed and finely sliced
>
> 1 dessertspoon sunflower oil
>
> 1 tablespoon light malt vinegar
>
> 1 teaspoon soy sauce
>
> 1 teaspoon chives
>
> black pepper

Cook the rice, drain and set aside. Heat the oil in a saucepan and gently fry the carrot. Remove from the heat and stir in the cooked rice and remaining ingredients. Mix thoroughly, transfer to a covered bowl and keep in the fridge.

Beetroot, apple and raisin salad *Serves 6*

> 1lb/450g beetroot, peeled and grated
>
> 8oz/225g eating apple, peeled, cored and grated
>
> 2oz/50g raisins
>
> 8 fl.oz/225ml fresh apple juice
>
> 1 teaspoon sunflower oil
>
> 1 dessertspoon white wine vinegar

Put the beetroot, raisins and apple juice in a saucepan and bring to the boil. Cover and simmer for about 15 minutes, until the juice has been absorbed, stirring frequently to prevent sticking. Remove from the heat and stir in the apple. Mix the sunflower oil with the vinegar and pour over the salad. Combine well and transfer the salad to a serving bowl. Cover and chill for a couple of hours before serving.

Cabbage, pineapple and date salad *Serves 6*

12oz/350g Chinese cabbage, finely shredded

4 tinned pineapple rings

4oz/100g dried dates, sliced

4oz/100g cucumber, cut into julienne strips

1oz/25g pumpkin seeds

6 spring onions, chopped

1 dessertspoon sunflower oil

1 teaspoon soy sauce

2 dessertspoons fresh pineapple juice

fresh coriander leaves

Pat the pineapple rings dry on kitchen paper, then chop them finely. Put them into a bowl with the Chinese cabbage, dates, cucumber, pumpkin seeds and spring onions. Mix the sunflower oil with the soy sauce and pineapple juice and pour it over the salad. Toss well. Garnish with fresh coriander leaves.

Mangetout, mushroom and sweetcorn salad *Serves 4*

4oz/100g mangetout, topped and tailed

2oz/50g button mushrooms, wiped and sliced

2oz/50g sweetcorn kernels, blanched

4 spring onions, trimmed and sliced

1 tablespoon white wine vinegar

1 teaspoon olive oil

1 teaspoon chives

black pepper

Cut the mangetout into ½ inch/1cm slices and steam until just tender. Rinse under a cold running tap, drain well and place in a bowl with the mushrooms, sweetcorn, spring onions and chives. Mix the olive oil with the vinegar and pour over the salad. Season with black pepper and toss. Transfer to a serving bowl, cover and chill.

Mexican salad *Serves 4*

2 avocado pears, peeled, stoned and diced

8oz/225g tomatoes, skinned and chopped

4oz/100g cooked red kidney beans

4oz/100g cooked sweetcorn kernels

4oz/100g red pepper, finely chopped

4 spring onions, trimmed and finely sliced

1 garlic clove, crushed

2 dessertspoons lemon juice

2 teaspoons olive oil

2 teaspoons oregano

2 teaspoons marjoram

pinch of chilli powder

dash of tabasco sauce

black pepper

crisp shredded lettuce leaves

fresh parsley

Put the avocados, tomatoes, kidney beans, sweetcorn, red pepper, spring onions and garlic in a bowl and stir. Mix the olive oil with the lemon juice and tabasco and add to the salad together with the oregano, marjoram and chilli powder. Season with black pepper and toss thoroughly. Arrange some shredded lettuce leaves on a serving plate, pile the salad on top and garnish with fresh parsley sprigs.

Mixed bean and barley salad *Serves 6*

8oz/225g frozen broad beans

8oz/225g mixed cooked beans (a mixture of black-eye, kidney, borlotti, flageolet etc.)

4oz/100g pot barley

2oz/50g red pepper, finely chopped

2oz/50g cucumber, finely chopped

4 spring onions, trimmed and finely sliced

1 dessertspoon sunflower oil

1 dessertspoon soy sauce

2 dessertspoons light malt vinegar

Boil the pot barley until cooked, drain and rinse under cold water. Drain well and transfer to a mixing bowl. Steam the broad beans until just tender and add to the barley together with the mixed beans, red pepper, cucumber and spring onions. Mix the sunflower oil with the soy sauce and vinegar and pour over the salad. Toss well and transfer to a serving bowl. Cover and chill.

Chickpea tabbouleh *Serves 4/6*

8oz/225g cooked chickpeas

4oz/100g bulgar wheat

10 fl.oz/300ml boiling water

1/2 teaspoon yeast extract

4 spring onions, trimmed and finely sliced

4 gherkins, finely chopped

4 rounded tablespoons finely chopped fresh mint

black pepper

1 dessertspoon olive oil

2 dessertspoons lemon juice

crips lettuce leaves

cucumber and tomato slices

fresh mint leaves

Dissolve the yeast extract in the water. Add the bulgar wheat, stir and allow to stand for 20 minutes. Put the soaked bulgar in a fine sieve or piece of muslin and squeeze out excess water. Transfer to a bowl and add the chickpeas, spring onions, gherkins and chopped mint. Season with black pepper and stir well. Mix the olive oil with the lemon juice and pour over the salad. Toss thoroughly, cover and put in the fridge for a couple of hours until cold.

Arrange some crisp lettuce leaves on a serving plate and spoon the salad onto the leaves. Garnish with cucumber and tomato slices and fresh mint leaves.

Chinese leaf, satsuma and raisin slaw *Serves 6*

1lb/450g Chinese leaves, finely shredded

2 satsumas, peeled and chopped

4oz/100g raisins

4 rounded tablespoons vegan mayonnaise substitute

2 dessertspoons fresh orange juice

1 dessertspoon cider vinegar

$1/4$ teaspoon ground cinnamon

$1/4$ teaspoon ground coriander

1 satsuma, peeled and segmented

Put the shredded Chinese leaves, chopped satsuma and raisins into a mixing bowl. Mix the mayonnaise substitute with the orange juice, vinegar, cinnamon and coriander. Spoon over the salad and toss. Transfer to a serving dish, cover and chill. Garnish with satsuma segments.

Red onion and kidney bean salad *Serves 4*

8oz/225g red onion, peeled

4oz/100g cooked red kidney beans

4oz/100g tomatoes, skinned and chopped

1 tablespoon olive oil

1 teaspoon white wine vinegar

1 teaspoon chervil

black pepper

chopped fresh parsley

Slice off a few onion rings and keep for garnish. Chop the remaining onions and fry in the olive oil for about 5 minutes until just beginning to soften. Add the tomatoes and cook for about 2 minutes until the tomatoes become pulpy. Remove from the heat and add the kidney beans, vinegar and chervil, season with black pepper and mix well. Put in a serving bowl, cover and chill for a couple of hours. Garnish with the onion rings and chopped parsley.

Potato and pesto salad   *Serves 4*

1¹/₂ lb/675g new potatoes, scraped

2 spring onions, trimmed and finely sliced

4 rounded tablespoons vegan natural yoghurt

2 rounded teaspoons pesto

black pepper

fresh basil leaves

Boil the potatoes, drain and rinse under cold running water. Drain the potatoes well and dice them. Put them in a bowl with the spring onions and season with black pepper. Mix the pesto with the yoghurt until smoooth and spoon it over the potatoes. Carefully stir the salad, then transfer it to a serving dish. Garnish with fresh basil leaves, cover and chill before serving.

SPREADS

S AVOURY SPREADS CAN BE USED WITH CRUSTY WHOLEMEAL BREAD, rolls or savoury biscuits, as sandwich fillings or to fill vol-au-vents.

Avocado and pumpkin seed

2 small or 1 large avocado pear, peeled and stoned

2oz/50g pumpkin seeds, ground

1 rounded tablespoon yeast flakes

1 teaspoon lemon juice

1 rounded teaspoon parsley

black pepper

Mash the avocado with the lemon juice. Add the remaining ingredients and mix thoroughly. To avoid discolouration, make this spread just before required.

Tofu and walnut

4oz/100g plain tofu, mashed

4oz/100g walnuts, grated

2 rounded tablespoons light tahini

1 teaspoon soy sauce

black pepper

Mix all the ingredients until well combined.

Watercress and soya bean

1 bunch of watercress, trimmed and finely chopped

8oz/225g cooked soya beans, mashed

2 rounded dessertspoons vegan tartare sauce

black pepper

Combine all the ingredients thoroughly.

Chickpea and parsley

8oz/225g cooked chickpeas, mashed

2oz/50g fresh parsley, finely chopped

2 spring onions, trimmed and finely chopped

2 rounded tablespoons light tahini

$1/2$ teaspoon yeast extract

black pepper

Mix the ingredients well.

Cashew nut and lentil

4oz/100g red lentils

3oz/75g cashew nuts, grated

2 rounded tablespoons cashew nut butter

1 teaspoon soy sauce

black pepper

Toast the grated cashew nuts until golden, then allow to cool. Cook the lentils until soft and drain them in a fine sieve, pressing out as much water as possible with the back of a spoon. Keep some of the cooking water. Put the lentils in a covered dish in the fridge until cold.

SALADS

NOT ONLY DO SALADS LOOK GOOD, THEY ARE ALSO PACKED WITH vitamins and minerals, as vegetables, fruits, nuts, beans, pulses, pasta and grains can all be made into salads. Most are very easy to prepare and can be served with main courses and buffet meals at any time of the year. Choose the freshest ingredients available and prepare salads no more than a couple of hours before required.

Pineapple and pistachio rice salad *Serves 4*

4oz/100g long grain brown rice

4oz/100g peeled fresh pineapple, finely chopped

1oz/25g pistachios, chopped

2 spring onions, trimmed and finely sliced

1 dessertspoon sunflower oil

10 fl.oz/300ml water

1/4 teaspoon turmeric

1 teaspoon chervil

black pepper

chopped fresh parsley

Heat the oil in a saucepan and gently fry the spring onions and rice for 2 minutes. Add the turmeric, chervil and water and season with black pepper. Stir well and bring to the boil, cover and simmer gently until the liquid has been absorbed and the rice is cooked. Put in a lidded container and refrigerate until cold. Fork through the rice and add the pineapple and pistachios. Mix well and transfer to a serving dish. Garnish with chopped fresh parsley.

Asparagus and pumpkin seed flan Serves 6

12oz/350g asparagus, trimmed

1 onion, peeled and finely chopped

4 fl.oz/125ml water

4 fl.oz/125ml soya milk

2oz/50g pumpkin seeds, ground

2oz/50g fresh wholemeal breadcrumbs

1 rounded tablespoon cornflour

1 tablespoon olive oil

1/4 teaspoon celery seed

1/2 teaspoon yeast extract

1/2 teaspoon thyme

black pepper

extra pumpkin seeds

Cut the top 2 inches/5cm of tip from each asparagus stalk and set aside. Finely chop the remaining stalks and fry with the onion in the olive oil for 5 minutes. Add the water, celery seed, yeast extract and thyme and season with black pepper. Bring to the boil, cover and simmer for about 10 minutes until tender. Transfer to a liquidiser with half the soya milk. Blend until smooth then return to the saucepan. Mix the cornflour with the remaining soya milk until smooth, and add to the puree. Stir well. Bring to the boil whilst stirring for a few seconds until the mixture thickens. Remove from the heat and add the breadcrumbs and ground pumpkin seeds. Steam the asparagus tips until just tender, cut them into 1 inch/2cm lengths and add to the mixture. Spoon the filling evenly into the pastry case and sprinkle the top with pumpkin seeds. Bake in a preheated oven at 180°C/350°F/Gas mark 4 for approximately 30 minutes more.

Asparagus and pumpkin seed flan *Serves 6*

12oz/350g asparagus, trimmed

1 onion, peeled and finely chopped

4 fl.oz/125ml water

4 fl.oz/125ml soya milk

2oz/50g pumpkin seeds, ground

2oz/50g fresh wholemeal breadcrumbs

1 rounded tablespoon cornflour

1 tablespoon olive oil

1/4 teaspoon celery seed

1/4 teaspoon yeast extract

1/2 teaspoon thyme

black pepper

extra pumpkin seeds

Cut the top 2 inches/5cm of tip from each asparagus stalk and set aside. Finely chop the remaining stalks and fry with the onion in the olive oil for 5 minutes. Add the water, celery seed, yeast extract and thyme and season with black pepper. Bring to the boil, cover and simmer for about 10 minutes until tender. Transfer to a liquidiser with half the soya milk. Blend until smooth then return to the saucepan. Mix the cornflour with the remaining soya milk until smooth, and add to the purée. Stir well. Bring to the boil whilst stirring for a few seconds until the mixture thickens. Remove from the heat and add the breadcrumbs and ground pumpkin seeds. Steam the asparagus tips until just tender, cut them into 1/2 inch/1cm lengths and add to the mixture. Spoon the filling evenly into the pastry case and sprinkle the top with pumpkin seeds. Bake in a preheated oven at 180°C/350°F/Gas mark 4 for approximately 30 minutes more.

Mix the toasted cashew nuts, cashew nut butter and soy sauce with the lentils. Season with black pepper and stir in a little of the cooking water until the mixture becomes spreadable.

Pinto bean and pistachio

4oz/100g pinto beans, mashed

2oz/50g pistachios, grated

1 rounded tablespoon light tahini

2 tablespoons soya milk

1 teaspoon balsamic vinegar

$1/4$ teaspoon paprika

black pepper

Mix all the ingredients until they are well combined.

Creamy kidney bean and mixed nut

6oz/175g cooked red kidney beans

3oz/75g vegan 'cream cheese'

$1^1/2$ oz/40g mixed nuts, grated

1 tablespoon sunflower oil

1 tablespoon soya milk

1 dessertspoon balsamic vinegar

$1/2$ teaspoon paprika

black pepper

Blend the kidney beans with the cream 'cheese', sunflower oil, soya milk, balsamic vinegar and paprika. Add the nuts and season with black pepper. Mix thoroughly.

Mushroom, sunflower and garlic

4oz/100g mushrooms, wiped and finely chopped

4oz/100g sunflower seeds, ground

2 garlic cloves, crushed

1 tablespoon olive oil

1 rounded tablespoon sunflower spread

2 tablespoons water

1 teaspoon soy sauce

black pepper

Heat the oil in a saucepan and gently fry the mushrooms and garlic for a couple of minutes until the juices begin to run. Remove from the heat and stir in the ground sunflower seeds. Add the remaining ingredients and mix very well.

RICE TIMBALES

To make little rice timbales, spoon the hot cooked rice into individual oiled ramekin dishes. Press the rice down firmly, cover and put in the fridge until cold. Slide a sharp knife around the edges, carefully invert the timbales onto a serving plate and add the garnish.

Lemon and ginger *Makes 8*

8oz/225g long grain rice

1oz/25g root ginger, peeled and finely chopped

$1/2$ oz/15g lemon grass, finely chopped

20 fl.oz/600ml water

1 tablespoon olive oil

2 dessertspoons lemon juice

black pepper

finely grated lemon peel

Heat the oil in a saucepan and gently fry the ginger and lemon grass for a couple of minutes. Add the rice and stir around for another minute. Add the water and lemon juice and season with black pepper. Stir well and bring to the boil. Cover and simmer until the liquid has been absorbed. Divide the rice between the ramekin dishes.

Garnish each timbale with a little grated lemon peel.

Mixed pepper and pesto *Makes 8*

1lb/450g mixed peppers (red, green, yellow, orange), finely
chopped

8oz/225g arborio rice

2 garlic cloves, crushed

2 tablespoons olive oil

1 tablespoon vegan pesto

1 tablespoon vegan 'parmesan' style seasoning

20 fl.oz/600ml water

black pepper

fresh parsley

Heat the oil in a saucepan and fry the mixed peppers and garlic for 5 minutes. Add the rice and fry for 1 minute, then the pesto and water and season with black pepper. Stir well and bring to the boil. Cover and simmer until the liquid has been absorbed. Remove from the heat and stir in the 'parmesan' style seasoning. Spoon the rice into the dishes. Garnish with sprigs of fresh parsley when serving.

Watercress and wild rice *Makes 8*

8oz/225g mixed long grain brown and wild rice

1 bunch of watercress, trimmed and finely chopped

20 fl.oz/600ml water

1 onion, peeled and grated

2 garlic cloves, crushed

1 tablespoon vegetable oil

1 teaspoon parsley

black pepper

watercress leaves

Heat the oil in a saucepan and fry the onion and garlic until soft. Add the rice and fry for 1 minute more. Blend the chopped watercress with the water until smooth and add to the pan together with the parsley. Season with black pepper and stir. Bring to the boil, cover and simmer until the liquid has been absorbed. Spoon into the ramekin dishes. Garnish each timbale with a couple of watercress leaves.

Tomato and basil *Makes 8*

8oz/225g long grain rice

1 onion, peeled and grated

1 tablespoon olive oil

2 rounded tablespoons tomato purée

2 rounded tablespoons finely chopped fresh basil

20 fl.oz/600ml water

black pepper

1 large tomato, cut into wedges

Heat the oil in a saucepan and gently fry the onion. Add the rice and fry for a further minute. Add the remaining ingredients apart from the tomato wedges, and stir well. Bring to the boil, cover and simmer until the liquid has been absorbed. Divide the rice between the dishes. Garnish with a tomato wedge each.

Carrot and coriander   *Makes 8*

8oz/225g long grain brown rice

8oz/225g carrot, scraped and grated

3 rounded tablespoons chopped fresh coriander

1 tablespoon vegetable oil

1 teaspoon paprika

black pepper

24 fl.oz./725ml water

fresh coriander leaves

Heat the oil in a saucepan and fry the rice and carrot for 2 minutes. Add the chopped coriander, paprika and water and season with black pepper. Stir well and bring to the boil. Cover and simmer until the liquid has been absorbed. Spoon into the dishes. Garnish each timbale with a fresh coriander leaf.

DIPS

Dips served with a selection of crudités make an interesting addition to the buffet spread. To prepare the crudités, simply wash, scrape or peel the vegetables and cut them into strips or chunks. Allow approximately 1½ lb/ 675g of mixed vegetables for 8 servings. Arrange the crudités around the bowl containing the dip on a serving plate. Each dip serves 8.

Red pepper and cranberry

8oz/225g red pepper, chopped

4oz/100g cranberry sauce

1 tomato, skinned and chopped

1 small onion, peeled and chopped

4 tablespoons water

1 tablespoon vegetable oil

$\frac{1}{2}$ teaspoon paprika

few drops of tabasco sauce

black pepper

Heat the oil in a saucepan and fry the pepper and onion until soft. Add the tomato, water, paprika and tabasco sauce and season with black pepper. Cook gently for a couple of minutes until the tomato becomes pulpy. Remove from the heat and allow to cool slightly, then transfer to a blender and add the cranberry sauce. Blend until smooth and pour into a serving bowl. Cover and chill before serving.

Creamy asparagus

1lb/450g asparagus, trimmed

8oz/225g vegan 'cream cheese'

pinch of ground bay leaves

black pepper

Steam the asparagus until tender, rinse under cold water and drain. Chop finely and blend until smooth with the 'cream cheese'. Add the ground bay leaves and season with black pepper. Mix well and transfer to a serving bowl. Cover and keep in the fridge until cold.

Watercress and walnut

1 bunch of watercress, trimmed and finely chopped

8oz/225g vegan 'cream cheese'

5oz/150ml pot natural soya yoghurt

2oz/50g walnuts, grated

1 teaspoon chives

black pepper

Mix all the ingredients thoroughly. Put in a serving dish, cover and chill.

Red lentil and tomato

8oz/225g tomatoes, skinned and chopped

4oz/100g red lentils

14 fl.oz/400ml water

1 onion, peeled and grated

1 garlic clove, crushed

1 tablespoon vegetable oil

1 dessertspoon tomato purée

1 teaspoon ground coriander

1 teaspoon ground cumin

pinch of chilli powder

black pepper

Heat the oil in a saucepan and gently fry the onion and garlic. Add the coriander, cumin and chilli powder and stir around for a few seconds. Raise the heat, add the tomatoes and cook until pulpy. Wash and drain the lentils and add to the pan together with the water. Season with black pepper and stir well. Bring to the boil, cover and simmer for about 35 minutes until the lentils are tender and the mixture is thick, stirring frequently to prevent sticking. Remove from the heat and mash with a potato masher. Stir well, pour into a serving bowl, cover and refrigerate.

Carrot and apricot

1lb/450g carrots, scraped and chopped

3oz/75g dried apricots

6 fl.oz/175ml water

$1/4$ teaspoon ground mace

5 fl.oz/150ml fresh apricot or orange juice

Chop the apricots finely and put them in a saucepan with the water. Bring to the boil and simmer until the apricots are pulpy and the mixture thickens. Steam the carrots until tender and put them in a blender with the apricots, mace and fruit juice. Blend until smooth, then transfer to a serving bowl. Put in the fridge to get cold.

Avocado and tomato

2 ripe avocado pears, peeled, stoned and chopped

4oz/100g tomatoes, skinned and finely chopped

1 garlic clove, crushed

1 dessertspoon lemon juice

2 dessertspoons olive oil

2 teaspoons chives

black pepper

Put all ingredients in a mixing bowl and mash with a potato masher until smooth. Transfer to a serving bowl, cover and chill.

Peanut and raisin

4 rounded tablespoons crunchy peanut butter

2oz/50g raisins, finely chopped

6 rounded tablespoons natural soya yoghurt

4oz/100g vegan 'cream cheese'

1 teaspoon soy sauce

black pepper

Mix all ingredients thoroughly. Transfer to a serving bowl, cover and refrigerate.

LITTLE SAVOURIES

These little finger foods are ideal for handing round with drinks or serving at a buffet spread. Apart from the *Garlic and sesame triangle toasties* and *Spicy mixed nuts*, they can all be made beforehand and frozen.

Walnut felafel *Makes approx. 14*

8oz/225g cooked chick peas, mashed

2oz/50g walnuts, grated

2oz/50g fresh wholemeal breadcrumbs

1 onion, peeled and grated

1 garlic clove, crushed

1 rounded tablespoon light tahini

1 tablespoon fresh lemon juice

1 dessertspoon sunflower oil

1 teaspoon soy sauce

$1/2$ teaspoon paprika

$1/2$ teaspoon ground cumin

$1/2$ teaspoon ground coriander

black pepper

sesame seeds

Heat the oil in a large saucepan and fry the onion and garlic until softened. Add the paprika, cumin and coriander and stir around for a few seconds, then remove from the heat and add all remaining ingredients except the sesame seeds. Mix thoroughly. Take rounded dessertspoonfuls of the mixture and roll into balls in the palm of the hand. Roll each ball in sesame seeds and place on a greased baking sheet. Bake in a preheated oven at 180°C/350°F/Gas mark 4 for about 25 minutes until golden. Turn once during cooking to ensure even browning. Serve either hot or cold.

Smoked tofu, walnut and sesame bites *Makes approx. 12*

8oz/225g smoked tofu, mashed

2oz/50g walnuts, grated

2oz/50g fresh wholemeal breadcrumbs

1 onion, peeled and finely chopped

1 tablespoon vegetable oil

1 rounded tablespoon light tahini

1 tablespoon soya milk

1 teaspoon parsley

1 teaspoon chervil

1 teaspoon soy sauce

black pepper

sesame seeds

Heat the oil in a saucepan and gently fry the onion until soft. Remove from the heat and stir in the tofu, walnuts, breadcrumbs, parsley and chervil. Mix the tahini with the soya milk and soy sauce until smooth. Add to the pan and season with black pepper. Mix thoroughly until the mixture binds together. Take heaped dessertspoonfuls of the mixture and roll into balls, then roll each ball in sesame seeds until completely covered. Place the balls on a greased baking sheet and bake in a preheated oven at 180°C/350°F/Gas mark 4 for approximately 25 minutes until golden brown, turning once. Serve either hot or cold.

Tahini, date and pecan nut rolls *Makes approx. 12*

4 rounded tablespoons light tahini

3oz/75g dried dates, finely chopped

3oz/75g pecans, grated

3oz/75g fresh wholemeal breadcrumbs

1/2 teaspoon ground coriander

1/4 teaspoon paprika

black pepper

sesame seeds

Put the dates, pecans, breadcrumbs, coriander and paprika in a bowl. Season with black pepper and stir. Add the tahini and mix thoroughly until the ingredients bind together. Take heaped dessertspoonfuls of the mixture and shape into little rolls. Roll each portion in sesame seeds until completely coated. Put the rolls on a plate, cover and keep in the fridge for a few hours before serving.

Herby hazelnut buttons *Makes approx. 50*

2oz/50g hazelnuts, finely chopped

2oz/50g fine wholemeal self raising flour

2oz/50g vegan 'cream cheese'

1oz/25g vegan margarine

1oz/25g oatbran

1 teaspoon mixed herbs

1/2 teaspoon paprika

black pepper

Cream the margarine with the 'cream cheese'. Add the remaining ingredients and mix thoroughly until a soft dough forms. Turn out onto a floured board and roll out to about 1/2 inch/1cm thick. Cut into 1 inch/2.5cm rounds using a cocktail cutter. Gather up and re-roll the dough until it is all used up. Place the buttons on a greased baking sheet and bake in a preheated oven at 180°C/350°F/Gas mark 4 for approximately 12 minutes until golden brown. Transfer to a wire rack and allow to cool.

Tofu, ginger and sesame cubes *Makes approx. 25*

8oz/225g marinated tofu, mashed

3oz/75g fresh wholemeal breadcrumbs

1oz/25g soya flour

1/2 oz/15g fresh root ginger, finely chopped

1 onion, peeled and finely chopped

2 tablespoons soya milk

1 tablespoon sunflower oil

1 rounded tablespoon light tahini

1 teaspoon soy sauce

1/2 teaspoon paprika

black pepper

sesame seeds

Heat the oil in a saucepan and gently fry the onion and ginger. Remove from the heat and add all remaining ingredients apart from the sesame seeds. Mix well, then take heaped teaspoonfuls of the mixture and shape into cubes. Press each side of the cubes in sesame seeds until completely covered. Transfer to a greased baking sheet and bake in a preheated oven at 180°C/350°F/Gas mark 4 for 20-25 minutes until golden. Serve either warm or cold.

Creamy pistachio-stuffed dates *Makes 20*

20 dessert dates, stoned

4oz/100g vegan 'cream cheese'

2oz/50g pistachios, finely grated

1 teaspoon balsamic vinegar

black pepper

Mix the 'cream cheese' with the grated pistachios and vinegar, season with black pepper and combine well. Stuff each of the dessert dates with about a rounded teaspoonful of the mixture and chill before serving.

Sunflower and sultana savouries *Makes approx. 20*

4oz/100g sunflower seeds, ground

2oz/50g vegan 'cream cheese'

2oz/50g sultanas, finely chopped

1oz/25g cream crackers, ground

$1/2$ teaspoon yeast extract

black pepper

$1/2$ oz/15g sunflower seeds, ground

Put the ingredients except the ½ oz/15g ground sunflower seeds into a bowl and mix thoroughly until the mixture binds. Take heaped teaspoonfuls and shape into balls. Roll each ball in the remaining ground sunflower seeds until completely covered. Put on a plate, cover and keep in the fridge for a few hours.

Spicy mixed nuts

8oz/225g mixed shelled nuts

1 tablespoon vegetable oil

1/2 teaspoon ground cumin

1/2 teaspoon ground coriander

1/2 teaspoon paprika

1/4 teaspoon turmeric

black pepper

Mix the oil with the spices and pour it into a shallow baking tin. Roughly chop the nuts and add them to the tin. Season with black pepper and stir until the nuts are well coated. Bake in a preheated oven at 170°C/325°F/Gas mark 3 for 15-20 minutes, stirring occasionally to ensure even browning. Allow to cool and transfer to a serving bowl.

Garlic and sesame triangle toasties

8 large (square) slices of medium-cut wholemeal bread

1 1/2 oz/40g vegan margarine

2 garlic cloves, crushed

sesame seeds

Cut the crusts off the slices of bread. Mix the garlic with the margarine and spread onto one side of each slice of bread. Sprinkle with sesame seeds and cut each slice into eight triangles. Place the triangles on a baking sheet and bake in a preheated oven at 180°C/350°F/Gas mark 4 for about 5 minutes until golden, then turn them over and bake for a further 5 minutes. Allow to cool on a wire rack.

Sunflower seed oaties *Makes approx. 24*

4oz/100g fine oatmeal

2oz/50g sunflower seeds, ground

2oz/50g fine wholemeal self raising flour

2oz/50g vegan margarine

1 rounded tablespoon sunflower spread

1 teaspoon soy sauce

approx. 3 tablespoons soya milk

Cream the margarine with the sunflower spread and soy sauce. Work in the oatmeal, ground sunflower seeds and flour, and gradually add the soya milk until a soft dough forms.

Turn out onto a floured board and roll out to about ¼inch/6mm thick. Cut into 2¼ inch/5½ cm rounds with a biscuit cutter. Carefully transfer the rounds to a greased baking sheet. Gather up and re-roll the dough until it is all used up. Bake in a preheated oven at 180°C/350°F/Gas mark 4 for approximately 10 minutes until golden brown. Carefully transfer the oaties to a wire rack to cool.

Pesto and pecan rolls *Makes 16*

1lb/450g plain wholemeal flour

¼ oz/7g sachet easy-blend yeast

2oz/50g vegan margarine

1oz/25g pecans, finely chopped

2 tablespoons olive oil

2 tablespoons vegan pesto

approx. 8 fl.oz/225ml warm water

soya milk

Mix the flour with the yeast and rub in the margarine. Blend the pesto with the olive oil and add to the bowl together with the pecans. Gradually add the water until the mixture binds together. Knead the dough, then return it to the bowl. Cover and leave in a warm place for 1 hour to rise. Knead the dough again and divide into sixteen equal portions. Roll each portion into a ball and place on a greased baking sheet. Leave in a warm place for 30 minutes. Brush with soya milk and bake in a preheated oven at 180°C/350°F/Gas mark 4 for about 18 minutes until golden brown. Allow to cool on a wire rack. Slice each roll in half and spread with vegan margarine or a savoury spread.

Mini sage and onion scones *Makes 12*

8oz/225g fine wholemeal self raising flour

2oz/50g vegan margarine

1 onion, peeled and grated

1 tablespoon olive oil

1 dessertspoon sage

approx. 3 fl.oz/75ml soya milk

extra soya milk

black onion seeds

Fry the onion in the olive oil until softened. Mix the sage with the flour and rub in the margarine. Stir in the onion and gradually add the soya milk until a soft dough forms. Turn out onto a floured board and roll out to approximately 5⁄8 inch/1½ cm thick. Cut into 2 inch/5cm rounds using a pastry cutter. Gather up the remaining dough and re-roll until it is used up.

Put the scones on a greased baking sheet. Brush the tops with soya milk and sprinkle with black onion seeds. Bake in a preheated oven at 170°C/325°F/Gas mark 3 for 15-20 minutes. Allow to cool on a wire rack. Cut the scones in half and spread with vegan margarine or a savoury spread.

Savoury vegetable and nut cakes *Makes 12*

4oz/100g fine wholemeal self raising flour

1oz/25g mushrooms, wiped

1oz/25g yellow pepper

1oz/25g red pepper

1oz/25g green pepper

1 small onion, peeled

1 garlic clove, crushed

$1/2$oz/15g soya flour

4 tablespoons water

4 tablespoons soya milk

1oz/25g vegan margarine

1oz/25g mixed nuts, finely chopped

1 rounded tablespoon sunflower spread

1 tablespoon olive oil

1 teaspoon parsley

$1/2$ teaspoon yeast extract

black pepper

sesame seeds

Finely chop the mushrooms, peppers and onion and fry with the garlic in the olive oil for 5 minutes. Add the sunflower spread, margarine and yeast extract and stir until melted. Remove from the heat. Whisk the soya flour with the water until smooth, then add to the pan together with the wholemeal flour, mixed nuts, parsley and soya milk. Season with black pepper and mix thoroughly. Divide the mixture between the holes of a greased 12-holed tart tin. Sprinkle with sesame seeds and bake in a preheated oven at 180°C/ 350°F/Gas mark 4 for 18-20 minutes until golden brown. Serve either warm or cold.

Nutty oatcakes *Makes 16*

3oz/75g porridge oats

3oz/75g medium oatmeal

2oz/50g fine wholemeal self raising flour

2oz/50g vegan margarine

1 rounded tablespoon mixed nut butter

4 tablespoons soya milk

Put the nut butter and margarine in a saucepan and heat until melted. Remove from the heat and stir in the porridge oats, oatmeal and flour. Add the soya milk and mix until a soft dough forms. Turn out onto a floured board and knead well. Divide the dough into sixteen equal portions and form each into a flat circular biscuit shape. Put the circles on a greased baking sheet and bake in a preheated oven at 180°C/350°F/Gas mark 4 for 15-18 minutes. Carefully transfer to a wire rack to cool.

DESSERTS

Tropical fruit jelly *Serves 6*

8oz/225g tin pineapple chunks in natural juice

1 passion fruit

1 ripe mango, peeled and diced

1 ripe paw paw, peeled and diced

4 kumquats, thinly sliced

tropical fruit juice

2 teaspoons agar agar

to serve
vegan yoghurt or ice cream

Strain the pineapple juice into a measuring jug and make up to 20 fl.oz/ 600ml with tropical fruit juice. Scoop the insides from the passion fruit and mix with the pineapple chunks, mango and paw paw. Transfer to a serving bowl.

Dissolve the agar agar in the fruit juice and heat gently whilst stirring until just below boiling point. Pour the juice over the fruit, cover and put in the fridge for a few hours until set. Garnish with the kumquat slices and serve with vegan yoghurt or ice cream.

Orange, date and mocha sundaes *Serves 4*

1 large or 2 small oranges

2oz/50g dried dates, finely chopped

20 fl.oz./600ml soya milk

2 rounded tablespoons custard powder

2 rounded tablespoons carob powder, sieved

1 rounded tablespoon demerara sugar

1 rounded dessertspoon coffee powder

1 teaspoon vanilla extract

4 squares orange-flavoured carob block, grated

Peel the orange and remove all pith and membranes. Chop the segments and mix with the dates. Divide the fruit between four sundae glasses. Grate a small amount of orange peel and keep it for garnishing.

Mix the custard powder, carob powder, sugar, coffee and vanilla extract with the soya milk and stir well until smooth. Transfer to a double boiler and bring to the boil whilst stirring. Continue stirring for a few seconds until the sauce thickens. Pour the sauce over the fruit in the glasses. Cover and refrigerate for a few hours until set. Sprinkle the grated carob on top and garnish with the grated orange peel.

Plum and coconut charlottes *Serves 4*

crumble mixture
2oz/50g fresh wholemeal breadcrumbs

1oz/25g desiccated coconut

3/4 oz/22g vegan margarine

1 dessertspoon demerara sugar

1/2 teaspoon ground cinnamon

filling
12oz/350g plums, stoned and chopped

1 rounded tablespoon demerara sugar

1 tablespoon fresh fruit juice

1 teaspoon arrowroot

Put the plums in a saucepan with the sugar and fruit juice, stir well and bring to the boil. Simmer gently until the plums are soft. Remove from the heat and stir in the arrowroot. Mix well until the arrowroot dissolves.

Melt the margarine in a saucepan. Add the remaining crumble ingredients and stir well. Cook for 3 minutes whilst stirring. Divide half the crumble mixture between four 3 inch/8cm diameter ramekin dishes. Press down firmly and evenly. Spoon the cooked plums over the crumble and sprinkle the remaining crumble mixture on top. Press down evenly, cover and put in the fridge until cold.

Summer fruit fool with granola *Serves 4*

3oz/75g strawberries

3oz/75g raspberries

2oz/50g blackcurrants

1oz/25g demerara sugar

2 tablespoons water

8 fl.oz/225ml sweetened soya milk

1 rounded tablespoon cornflour

topping

vegan granola

extra strawberries and raspberries

Put the strawberries, raspberries and blackcurrants in a saucepan with the sugar and water. Bring to the boil, cover and simmer for a few minutes until the fruit is soft. Mix the cornflour with the soya milk until smooth, pour this into a blender and add the cooked fruit. Blend until smooth, then pass the mixture through a sieve into a double boiler. Bring to the boil whilst stirring continuously. Pour the thickened mixture into four serving glasses. Cover and chill for a few hours. Top with granola and garnish with raspberries and halved strawberries when serving.

Maple, cherry and walnut trifle *Serves 8*

sponge

4oz/100g fine wholemeal self raising flour

2oz/50g vegan margarine

1oz/25g demerara sugar

1oz/25g walnuts, grated

1oz/25g glacé cherries, washed, dried and finely chopped

2 tablespoons maple syrup

5 fl.oz/150ml soya milk

filling

1lb/450g cherries, stoned

10 fl.oz/300ml apple juice

1 tablespoon demerara sugar

2 teaspoons agar agar

topping

20 fl.oz/600ml soya milk

2 tablespoons maple syrup

2 rounded tablespoons custard powder

1oz/25g walnuts, finely chopped

1oz/25g glacé cherries, washed, dried and halved

Cream the margarine with the sugar and maple syrup. Add the sifted flour, grated walnuts, chopped cherries and soya milk and mix thoroughly. Spoon the mixture into a lined and greased 7 inch/18cm diameter flan tin. Spread out evenly and bake in a preheated oven at 180°C/350°F/Gas mark 4 for approximately 20 minutes until golden. Turn out onto a wire rack and allow to cool. When cold, chop the sponge and put it in a serving bowl.

Bring the cherries, apple juice and sugar to the boil. Simmer for a couple of minutes until the cherries begin to soften. Strain the juice from the cherries and keep. Spoon the cherries over the sponge in the serving bowl. Dissolve the agar agar in the reserved juice and heat gently whilst stirring until just below boiling point. Pour the juice over the cherries, cover and keep in the fridge for a couple of hours until set.

Dissolve the custard powder and maple syrup in the soya milk. Transfer to a double boiler and bring to the boil whilst stirring. Continue stirring until the custard thickens. Pour over the cherries and jelly. Cover and return to the fridge for a few hours. Garnish with the chopped walnuts and halved cherries.

Index

Pastries

Salads

Spreads

Rice timbales

Dips

VEGAN DINNER PARTIES

Linda Majzlik

Foreword by Juliet Gellatley

All the recipes are tried and tested. Although they are organised into monthly menus, you can of course pick and choose to make up menus and dishes for any occasion.

Illustrated with cartoons by Mark Blanford, the book makes the perfect gift.

Also by **Linda Majzlik**: *Festive Food for Vegetarians* and *Party Food for Vegetarians*.

✓ 'For the sake of the world, its people and its animals, it is important to reclaim our food from those who pretend that pain and suffering are an essential part of our diet. Enjoy these great recipes because they strike a blow for the oppressed of the world — humans and animals alike.' From the Foreword by Juliet Gellatley, founder and director of Viva!

✓ 'This inspiring book proves just how sophisticated and tasty vegan food can be.' *Agscene*, Compassion in World Farming

£5 pbk 96pp 1 897766 46 7

ANIMAL CENTURY

A CELEBRATION OF CHANGING ATTITUDES TO ANIMALS

Mark Gold

The illustrated story of a century of animal liberation and welfare, told in the voices of many of the century's most prominent campaigners, against a backdrop of accelerating social and political change.

This is a social history that has been largely unwritten — until now. From the 'brown dog' who inspired riots on the streets of London to the Greenpeace campaign to 'save the whales'; from public praise for George V's slaughter of 21 Indian tigers to fierce criticism of Prince Charles for his support for hunting; from the birth of the conservation and wildlife protection movements to the passionate campaign to stop the live export of animals — *Animal Century* offers a fascinating insight into the events which changed our attitudes, and the people who made it all happen.

Includes interviews with Maneka Gandhi, Jane Goodall, Celia Hammond, Ali Hassani, Virginia McKenna, Peter Singer, Kathleen Jannaway, Sarah Kite, Ronnie Lee, Peter Roberts, Anthony Thomas, Dave Wetton and Irene Williams, plus many historic illustrations.

✓ 'Absolutely rivetting.' *Outrage*

✓ 'This is a wonderful book, an easy read and recommended to people who have an interest in the movement.' *The Vegetarian*

£12.99 pbk 240pp 1 897766 43 2

For a complete catalogue of our publications, including many titles distributed for other organisations,
please phone 01608 811969 or 01689 870437.